Los Ambulantes

The MIT Press
Cambridge, Massachusetts
London, England

Los Ambulantes

The Itinerant Photographers of Guatemala

photographs by Ann Parker
text by Avon Neal

This book was set in Futura by County Photo Composition Corp.,
printed by Rapoport Printing Corp., and bound by Halliday Lithograph
in the United States of America.

Library of Congress Cataloging in Publication Data

Parker, Ann.
   Los ambulantes: the itinerant photographers of Guatemala.

   1. Photography—Guatemala. 2. Photographers—Guatemala. I. Neal,
Avon. II. Title.
TR31.G9P37   770'.92'2   82-6526
ISBN 0-262-16086-2   AACR2

Contents

Preface

From that day in the spring of 1971 when I first chanced upon a group of itinerant photographers working with their old-fashioned cameras and painted backdrops in a Guatemalan marketplace I have been fascinated by their world and the images that pass before their lenses.

I am especially intrigued by the intensity with which Indians from highland villages react to being photographed in the manner of the itinerants. Their almost trancelike expressions, so reminiscent of the formal portraiture found on tintypes and daguerreotypes, clearly show that for them the camera still retains much of the powerful magic it had in its earliest years. In our society, where it is not uncommon for people to be photographed hundreds of times, the psychological impact of facing a camera is greatly diminished. Many of the people shown in this book were sitting in front of a camera for the first and perhaps only time. The casual snapshot plays no part in their existence, and the rarity of coming before a lens is reflected in the portraits. Even such softening details as the backdrops, the props, or the informality of a child's gesture seem to heighten rather than destroy the basic mood.

Over several years my husband Avon Neal and I have spent many weeks sharing the daily lives of *los ambulantes*. We have met them in the chill predawn hours and crowded with them onto buses jammed with Indian families and merchants bound for *la feria*, the annual fair, in some far-off mountain village. We have shared their elation on busy days and learned from their perseverance on slow and discouraging ones. As the weeks became months, as we traced and retraced familiar backroads and highways, as Indian words and place names began to have meaning, the materials for the book gradually came together.

While we traveled with these roving picture makers a day never passed without some magical blending of fantasy and reality within their tentlike stalls. It was like waiting before a series of small stages for unknown dramas to unfold. In one cubicle two country Indians stand transfixed before towering skyscrapers, the true likes of which they will probably never see; at another a wizened old lady commemorates her eighty-fourth birthday by serenely sharing her portrait with an ever-benevolent angel; a third backdrop, chosen for its boldly lettered sentiments, provides a remembrance for a young husband and wife and their tiny child as they stare solemnly into the camera's eye. From the fantasy worlds of their choice each will carry home a small but treasured image that when viewed in the days and months ahead, may become more real than the paper it is printed on.

The tradition of the itinerant photographer still flourishes in Guatemala, but in future decades it is sure to become another of the countless victims of economic progress. Already in many parts of the world where itinerants once roamed there are now only occasional park photographers, working without backdrops or props, photographing city dwellers on Sunday outings, to remind us of a lost, romantic past. Their subject matter pales before the exotica that continue to grace itinerants' lenses in the Guatemalan highlands.

If there existed a copy of every photograph taken by Guatemalan itinerants over the past few decades, if the photographers had been better trained and equipped, and if their pictures had not soon faded and yellowed, curators and social historians would have a significant archive from which to edit a collection of singular beauty. None of these "ifs" can be realized. The role of the itinerant photographer is simply to supply cheap photographs to the great majority of people who do not have access to and could not afford any other way. More is neither asked for nor received.

In a kind of partnership with the itinerants, I have acted as their photographic spokesman to record, in a more lasting way than they are able to, the essence of their world. I brought to the task my vision, my photographic knowledge and equipment, and my firm belief in the importance of recording this folk tradition. Avon Neal offered his skill as a writer, his patient research, and his constant companionship and encouragement, without which I might often have become disheartened. The photographers not only produced the environments and directed the events, but also extended their acceptance, their cooperation, and their warmth. The subjects, unaware of the part they were playing, gave the beauty of themselves.

Both Avon Neal and I thank the staff of the MIT Press, which brought the book from a dream to a reality with ease and graciousness, and the two anonymous donors without whose generosity the book would have suffered. We also thank the many people who offered help and friendship, opened their homes, and took the time to share some of their wide-ranging knowledge and experience of the beautiful but often mystifying land that is Guatemala.

Ann Parker
Thistle Hill, North Brookfield, Massachusetts

Photographs taken by itinerant
photographers, reproduced
in their original sizes. Included
is a portrait of the authors.

Chichicastenango

Santiago Atitlán

Nebaj

Sololá

Nebaj

Cobán

Huehuetenango

Joyabaj

Los Ambulantes

There still exists in many Latin American countries a picture-making tradition that reaches back to the earliest days of photography. The guardians of this colorful folk tradition are the itinerant photographers who follow secular and religious fairs from village to village, photographing people who might otherwise never face a camera. These men work in the old-fashioned manner of their predecessors, using much the same basic equipment that traveling photographers have relied upon for generations: a simple portable combination of view camera and darkroom, a plain wooden tripod, a painted backdrop, and a few standard props. Their fees are modest, and the photographs they take fulfill an emotional desire or an official necessity.

In most countries itinerant photographers have already disappeared. Better transportation, modern photographic techniques, and inexpensive cameras have greatly diminished their ranks. Of the hundreds who once roamed the dusty byroads of Mexico and Central America only a few score now practice as true itinerants; most have become studio or park photographers. Guatemala, where there is still a functional need for itinerants, is a notable exception. How long this tradition will continue depends largely upon the future economics of rural and village life. A relatively affluent populace buys simple cameras and takes its own snapshots, and for formal occasions it can afford the services of commercial studios.

In effect, the itinerant photographers of Guatemala are following a picture-making tradition that closely parallels the work of North America's early limners, who in their time created a whole new genre of folk painting. They are simply reproducing in a different medium the images of people who, for the sake of vanity or more practical reasons, want pictures of themselves or their loved ones.

It is customary for photographers to visit out-of-the-way places during saints' days and national holidays. (They are less active at Easter, when the people spend their money on candles and other religious articles and when many photographers who are also farmers are likely to be at home planting.) Along with their cameras and their flamboyant props, the *fotografos ambulantes* bring an air of mystery and romance. Most women come to the celebrations wearing the colorful costumes of their villages. The men, when not in native costume, usually wear dark suits and straw hats. A carnival atmosphere prevails, and money is spent with reckless abandon. This is the time to celebrate the past year's beneficence or to mourn its misfortunes, to purge one's soul and begin anew. Besides the traditional religious festivities there is much trading, buying and selling, general mixing, and matchmaking. In the evenings there is music, dancing, and drinking. It has become customary for celebrants to have their pictures taken as mementos. For about an average day's pay they can pose in front of a painted backdrop and be instantly transfigured by the camera's magic.

There are also practical reasons for having one's picture taken, and these constitute a considerable share of the photographer's work—especially when there is no local studio. As bureaucracy has encroached more and more on daily life, the demand for photographs has risen. Most common are the mundane photographs that accompany many official documents. An identification card, called a *cedula,* is technically required for every person over the age of eighteen. Itinerants provide the most economical and often the only means of obtaining the photographs required for various documents, such as organization membership cards, army conscription papers, and drivers' licenses.

Weddings and baptisms present good opportunities for photographers. Those who set up their cameras outside historic churches are doubly blessed, for they not only get the business of pilgrims wanting photographic keepsakes but are often called upon to record a wedding party. In most such instances the transaction is not prearranged. As a wedding group emerges from the church, the photographer hurries his camera onto the worn steps and positions the bride and groom so that the ornately carved facade provides an appropriate background. He works briskly to get his pictures, which are then processed and promptly delivered. If the prospect seems favorable, he may risk making several copies in the hope of multiple sales to the newlyweds' friends and relatives. The equivalent of fifty cents or a dollar is considered an ample reward for his labor, but with luck he may earn twice that amount. Within thirty minutes he is back at his post, ready for new customers.

Although the territory covered by most itinerants is limited to the marketplaces of towns and villages within a few hours of home, a photographer will sometimes travel the length and breadth of the land if he thinks he might turn a good profit. A few have even crossed the borders into neighboring countries—particularly Mexico, where for a small fee they can ply their trade without interference.

The itinerant photographer is distinguished from his urban, nontraveling counterpart chiefly by his habit of moving around the countryside. His working life revolves around the calendar of annual fairs. Whereas the studio photographer's patrons are drawn mostly from the middle and upper classes, the itinerant's are, with few exceptions, the Indians and local villagers who live in and around the areas where he has temporarily set up shop. The city photographer has a higher social standing than the itinerant, assuming the status and respectability of a professional. Although some itinerants aspire to set up studios, most seem content to follow the fairs. These itinerants admit that they would not know how to operate a fancy photography establishment. Some do maintain places of business, but these are relatively unpretentious, rarely approaching the luxury of a well-appointed studio.

Itinerants are not exempted from paying rent, however; each municipality levies a fee for the privilege of doing business within its precincts. This small fee is collected by an official who makes his daily rounds with a coin pouch and a sheaf of tickets printed on cheap paper. A photographer usually rents three meters of space to set up his booth. Prices vary from village to village, costing twenty, fifty, or seventy-five cents and up per meter. Momostenango, the blanket-weaving center, with its very active regional fairs, is the most expensive, with a set fee of $2.50 per designated workspace.

The itinerant's life is more difficult and less financially secure than the studio photographer's. It has a distinct flair of its own, a carefree rhythm that attracts certain temperaments and is reflected in the attitudes of the men themselves. Theirs is the gypsy-style world of the wanderers and the traveling circus and carnival folk. There is no excitement quite like that of a fair in full swing, when thousands of people crowd into a town and the sights and sounds of merriment are everywhere. It is then that a photographer's fortunes rise or fall. That is the gamble, the ultimate challenge, and the hope that keeps the itinerant going.

Some fairs are known to be more lucrative than others, but a photographer's success will vary from one year to the next. If crops have been good an itinerant may earn more than thirty dollars on the main day of a fair; if drought or pestilence has caused crop failures he may not even make his expenses.

It is estimated that there are approximately three hundred qualified photographers in all of Guatemala, of which about half operate as itinerants. These fall roughly into two basic groups, divided geographically. Those from the *Occidente* (the western division) work mainly in the highlands. Many live in or around Quezeltenango. An unusually large number of them are members of a few families and come from the nearby village of Olintepeque. The *Oriente* faction is concentrated in the area of Zacapa and covers fairs in the lowlands of eastern Guatemala. Between these two groups are about forty street and park photographers who reside in Guatemala City and occasionally travel to fairs in both directions.

In recent years, itinerants with *instantes*—Polaroid cameras—have begun to appear in city parks and at religious shrines to offer *fotos al minuto*. They have begun to turn up at fairs where there is the promise of people sophisticated enough to spend more money on this modern type of photograph. Those who work exclusively with *instantes* are usually young men from Guatemala City. They dress more stylishly and their manner is more aggressive. They tend to be smooth talkers and do not hesitate to solicit business. They appeal more to the *ladino* middle class, of which they are members. (*Ladino* corresponds roughly to the Mexican term *meztizo*—"mixed blood.") The more primitive Indians seem intimidated by their manner and appearance; besides, most could not afford their services. There appears to be little rivalry between the two camps of photographers. Each has its own particular clientele and knows from experience that the very subtle socioeconomic boundary lines are not easily breached.

Color is a major attraction of the Polaroid photograph, and the instant availability appeals to pleasure seekers on the move. The current price for a black-and-white Polaroid photograph is one *quetzal,* the equivalent of a dollar. This price is doubled for a photograph in color. A black-and-white picture of equal size from an itinerant would cost only half as much. For example, a customer can have a full postcard-size photograph, or two copies of the more popular half-postcard size, or four small *cedula*-type identity pictures for fifty *ling* (cents). Price is always determined by the size of the photograph, and it remains the same whether for an individual or a family group.

The men with *instantes* do not encumber themselves with the conventional painted backdrops, and prefer to solicit work by moving freely among the crowds. They pose their clients against walls, historic monuments, flowering shrubs, statues, or the ornate facades of colonial architecture; a much-favored setting is provided by the rows of ascending steps fronting the entrances of richly ornamented cathedrals.

In a land where tradition dies hard, Polaroid cameras have already demonstrated their practicality and are beginning to influence the attitudes of photographers and patrons. With the increase of affluence and sophistication the Polaroid may very well prove to be the next step in the evolution of itinerant photography, but the less expensive work of the traditional itinerants is still much more in demand at fairs and markets.

For many itinerants, photography is only a part-time occupation because there is simply not enough work to keep all of them profitably employed on a full-time basis. Some who live in urban areas have jobs that allow them only Sundays and holidays to pursue their photographic interests. Others are rural villagers who tend the soil and take up itinerancy between planting and harvesting or for special festivals.

When on the road, itinerants must plan their schedules carefully to cover the greatest number of fairs without unnecessary travel. They generally stay with friends or relatives or at cheap little boarding houses where they can store excess baggage and take occasional meals. By living this way they manage to keep their expenses to a minimum.

Since itinerants keep no records it is difficult to say what their annual earnings might be. To complicate matters, their individual estimates are so varied and unreliable that even a rough guess could be misleading; survival is about the only accurate measure of success in an occupation so dependent upon the whims of fortune. One of the more diligent photographers, reflecting over his life on the road, claimed that he had always made a good living, adding somewhat boastfully that any active itinerant could earn as much as $500 a year. If that figure sounds small, it must be remembered that such a sum is considerably above the average workingman's wage in present-day Guatemala.

One problem shared by all itinerants is that big fairs, particularly those for patron saints, often fall on the same dates in widely separated places. Business gained at one location will be lost at another. For maximum profit, a father and son may travel in different directions; otherwise a photographer may simply forgo a distant fair, knowing that others living in closer proximity will already have covered it.

Members of the same family often pursue the uncertain life of the traveling photographer. It is not unusual for fathers and sons, brothers, cousins, uncles, and nephews to work the fairs together. A younger person usually helps out as an apprentice until he learns the trade well enough to go into business for himself. By that time he has either constructed his own camera or purchased one from another photographer. His first backdrop is likely to be no more than a plain cloth or a crudely lettered curtain. He might work several seasons before he can afford to invest in a fancifully painted background or his own carved wooden horse. Once outfitted, the young man sets up with his colleagues, usually alongside the relative who instructed him. Just as veterans quietly leave the ranks, neophytes are accepted into the small community of itinerants without ceremony.

Of all marketplace practitioners the photographers seem the least mercenary or argumentative. This is probably due in part to their working with fixed prices, which precludes abrasive haggling.

Itinerant photographers are generally sober, hard-working men who have learned to accept the ups and downs of their calling. They are courteous to their clients, and most are congenial, cooperative, and ungrudgingly generous with each other. That some are Indians and others *ladinos* seems irrelevant. Their common bond, aside from family ties, has been forged from years of photographic experience and life on the road. One of their predominant characteristics is the light-hearted good humor displayed under what are sometimes exasperating conditions. Most are Catholics by heritage, but within their ranks a curiously disproportionate number have been baptized into one or another of the evangelical faiths that have proliferated in Central America during the past several decades—another indication that they tend to be individualistic and receptive to new ideas.

There were few good roads in Guatemala until the 1930s. Itinerants traveled the network of trails that crisscrossed Guatemala, southern Mexico, and the Yucatan. To get to their destinations they either walked or rode on horseback from the place where they left the train. Included in their rounds were the great ranch spreads, the *fincas* and *haciendas,* which hired hundreds of employees and were like villages unto themselves. Here the people turned out for *fiestas* and other celebrations and a photographer could spend several days taking pictures, ending up with a tidy profit.

One must always take into account when speaking of a country like Guatemala how terribly difficult it is for a rural Indian to rise above his condition, either economically or psychologically. For Indians who speak only dialect it is next to impossible. Although most itinerant photographers have had some degree of formal education and a few have made efforts to school themselves beyond the classroom, there are still those who can barely read or write. This is not a prerequisite to practicing their craft, but it does impose certain limitations and is sometimes a source of embarrassment when brought to light. A man may laboriously spell out his name in a hand that is hardly legible and still take good photographs and deal effectively with the public.

Only a small percentage of the itinerants are outstanding craftsmen. These are the ones who are imaginative as well as neat and careful in their ways of working. They strive to improve their techniques and equipment. Even though such qualifications are commendable, they do not necessarily impress prospective customers; other factors are involved in the client's final choice of a photographer.

In nearly all societies operating at a low economic level, festive holidays are events of singular importance. Among other things, they break the almost ritualized routine of day-to-day existence. Besides their social or religious functions, fairs and markets provide the common meeting ground for exchanging rural and city products. On such special days even the most ordinary marketplace is transformed. Throngs of Indians begin arriving before daylight, and by mid-morning the selling and bartering are at a peak. *Ladino* townspeople mingle with mountain Indians in crowded stores and plazas while they shop amid tantalizing displays of seasonal fruits and vegetables, pottery, hardware, clothing, and bolts of commercial cloth patterned after typical native designs.

In addition to photographers there is a whole nomadic army of hawkers and walkers who depend upon such places for a livelihood. From Momostenango come bands of blanket weavers bent under heavy bales of *serapes,* hand-woven jackets, and other woolen wear. Optimistic salesmen travel from the capital to bring more machine-made shoes, hats, jackets, and cotton yardage than they could sell at even the liveliest of fairs. Hardwaremongers appear with a jangling assortment of metal implements—hand tools, *machetes,* iron hinges, locks with keys, nails, cheap plastic toys, and even fish-shaped pocket knives imported from Germany. Carpenters come, too, lugging brightly painted wooden chests and cumbersome loads of hand-hewn furniture to be assembled on the spot. Dusty potters who have hiked over mountainous trails carrying tall racks of low-fired clay vessels spread their merchandise in neat rows on the cobbled streets. Candy vendors set up rickety stands or wander through milling crowds with garlands of gaily colored, husk-wrapped candy looped around their necks and arms. Patent-medicine salesmen hawk bottled elixirs and cure-alls by reciting in monotonous singsong a catalog of ailments as they parade up and down the aisles of merchants' stalls.

At the larger fairs some vendors sell from trucks parked on busy streets and market plazas. They bring coconuts from the hot coastal plain and great mounds of canta-loupes and watermelons from neighboring El Salvador. In the shade of canvas-covered truck beds women juggle weights and tend the scales as they dispense molded platters of crudely refined brown sugar.

Major fairs invariably attract sharp operators with beguiling schemes of skill and chance. There are carnival games of all kinds, including lotteries, penny pitches, bingo-type boards, and variations of the infamous shell game. Among the most popu-lar con artists are "birdmen," fortune tellers who go from fair to fair with cages of trained canaries and parakeets. At a signal the birds select with their beaks from pre-pared packets tiny slips of paper with fortunes printed on them. For this performance the owner rewards them with birdseed and is in turn rewarded with a few cents from his gullible client.

Ordinary market days are lively enough, but all community activity is greatly multi-plied on the occasion of a fair. If the celebration takes place near a main road that heavy trucks can navigate, it is probable that a Ferris wheel, a carousel, and other amusement machines will be installed. The more removed a fair is from urban centers the more likely it is to retain its old-fashioned character and to have the traditional processions, masked ceremonial dancers, and rituals. Nowadays practically all fairs have elements of both Indian and *ladino* celebration.

Highland fairs and market days in Guatemala are a melange of exotic sights, sounds, and smells. The noisy din and pulsating beat of the marketplace are every-where. During the dry season, cobblestoned streets literally vibrate under the glaring tropical sun. It is a fortunate day when merchants' sunshades are set billowing in the breeze. Village plazas generally become so hot and dusty by midday that people seek the shade of adobe walls or linger beneath the sagging awnings of market stalls.

Fairs go on in much the same manner during the country's rainy season. Participants (especially Indians) seem oblivious to precipitation, taking shelter only when they are drenched by blinding sheets of rain. Photographers stay set up and keep working through a steady drizzle, but with each sudden downpour they retreat to wait out the deluge in convenient doorways, beneath the plaza's bandstand, or under an ar-cade's protective arches. When no other shelter is available they join the merchants who, at the first flurry of raindrops, hurriedly cover themselves and their belongings with blanket-sized squares of plastic and huddle disconsolately beneath drooping, water-laden awnings as floods of runoff splash the cobblestones. Showers are usually short, but they come frequently enough to keep photographers busy fussing with the sheets of plastic that cover their props and cameras. If the downpour persists it can spoil their day completely.

The festivities continue even in driving rain. Ferris wheels take their leisurely turns, and primitive wooden carousels propelled by the treadmill labor of young boys continue their creaking rounds as the water beats down. Buildings swell with close-packed bodies, and strains of music drift from dark interiors throbbing with the muffled sounds of dancing. The rustle of crowd movement is everywhere. Voices lift from the unintelligible babble. The heady odor of mingled charcoal smoke and wet woolen-wear hangs over the whole assembly, and during the brief intervals of sun one can see wisps of steam rising from the chill-damp backs of Indians.

In places like lakeside Santiago Atitlan, where photographers say it rains at every summer fair, activity barely slackens as spectators wade ankle-deep through muddy puddles in densely crowded mazes that alternate between cobbled streets and torrential streams. In the most drenching downpour basketball games are played as enthusiastically as though the weather were clear while ceremonial fireworks are sent whizzing aloft from portable launching pads set up in front of the church. People attend fairs to enjoy themselves, and come rain or shine Guatemalan Indians make the most of their long-awaited opportunities.

On sunny days multitudes of bare and roughshod feet create a quick-step sibilance as they shuffle over worn cobblestones. Street cries, raucous shouts, and the shrill singsong of merchants peddling their wares dissolve into an overwhelming babble punctuated by the bleating of sheep, the explosive gobble of turkeys, the mooing of bewildered cattle, the frantic squawks of trussed-up chickens, and the squeals of tormented pigs as discriminating buyers probe and inspect them.

A cacophony of human voices and animal cries accompanies the ever-present music—strummed guitars, a blind man singing ballads, an ancient jukebox echoing from a *cantina* on the square, the raspy scratch of popular recordings blaring over a loudspeaker, and in country villages the primitive beat and hollow, tinny resonance of *marimbas*. Over the hubbub, dominating all things sacred and profane, drifts the clear, familiar sound of church bells summoning worshippers to the cool, dark interiors of peaceful sanctuaries.

Cascades of curious scents and smells flood every marketplace. In the early morning, clouds of pungent woodsmoke hang in blue layers above the area where traditional foods are cooked over open fires. The enticing aroma of steaming *chuchas,* fried meat, corn *tortillas,* and boiling coffee capture the essence of native breakfasts throughout the highlands. Among stirring market stalls a spicy fragrance of flowers, fruits, and garden produce spreads like perfume on the air. Incense is wafted from open churches, and where Indian rituals are in progress the smoke of *copal* (an aromatic pine-pitch resin) permeates the village. By mid-morning the streets have become undulating rivers of humanity as hordes of perspiring bodies press against each other and fill the narrow passageways. At every turn the acrid stench of raw wool and freshly cured leather assails one's nostrils. In the crowded transportation depots, animal odors blend with oily exhaust fumes from trucks and buses. Once experienced, these fairs and marketplaces instill a strange and compelling nostalgia that lingers long after the details have been forgotten.

For itinerant photographers, the principals of all fairs are the Indians who pour In from the surrounding hills and valleys. For centuries they and their forebears have traversed winding jungle trails, whole families and often entire communities walking for days to reach a favorite fair. They arrive in the early daylight hours at such centers as Barillas, Huehuetenango, San Francisco el Alto, Totonicapán, Sololá, and Chichicastenango with their burdens of pottery, avocados, firewood, and grain. Many lead domestic animals or drive pigs and sheep before them; others bring clusters of turkeys slung over their shoulders or chickens nestled in reed baskets balanced on top of their heads. Women carry eggs neatly gathered into folded leaves or corner-tied squares of faded cloth, along with herbs, handicrafts, flowers, and whatever else they can sell or trade. Each district contributes its own specialty. Men from Todos Santos are famous for potatoes; those from Nahualá specialize in woven bags and *metates,* the heavy, tri-legged stones concavely shaped for grinding corn. Farmers from villages around Lake Atitlán bring huge netlike bags of carrots, onions, and yams, and those from the lowlands bring pineapples, oranges, coconuts, and *zapotes.* Occasionally, lake people arrive with baskets of fish and freshwater crabs. They barter for necessities, visit with neighbors, pay their respects to the church, feast their eyes on a world of strange and wonderful sights, and sometimes—if they have had good luck in the marketplace—spend some hard-earned coins on photographs.

These crowds of visiting Indians, resplendent in their colorful costumes and jewelry, move along the bustling thoroughfare where itinerants have set up their cameras in a closely packed row of glittering temptations. Mothers with babes on their backs or at their breasts and with children in tow, awkward young men and bevies of giggling girls, and seam-faced old men and women pause to inspect the frames of posted pictures. They linger, trying to decide, commenting softly to one another when they recognize a familiar face. A few become customers; most are only curious.

The busiest time for photographers is during the celebration honoring a village's patron saint, which usually comes a day or two before the fair is officially over. Nevertheless, most photographers stay on for the duration unless there is a chance they can make it to another fair in time for its peak day. Some may try to return home between sessions, but during a lively season when saints' days and national holidays come close together they no sooner finish one fair before they must pack up and head for another. It is not unusual for an itinerant to work a market or a saint's-day fair, catch a late bus to a distant town, arrive by midnight, sleep a couple of hours, and have his backdrop unfurled and his camera ready by dawn, when the marketplace is beginning to stir. He may stay there until late afternoon, then hurry on to some far destination to be on hand for a three-day fair. Photographers know their schedules by heart; sometimes, as if at a prearranged signal, a dozen or more will converge on a festive village at the same time.

An itinerant photographer generally arrives at a work site on one of the many early-morning vehicles that transport farmers and their produce to the marketplace—usually an antiquated and overcrowded second- or third-class *autobus* that has rumbled, groaned, and rattled too long over Guatemala's dusty, rutted roads. Some of these are run-down minibuses or vans; others appear to be former school buses like those used in the United States. Bus companies choose such names as *Reina de Utatlán* (queen of Utatlán), *Condór, Fuente del Norte* (fountain of the North), and *Dalia Azul* (blue dahlia), but these romantic appelations have little to do with the quality of transportation. Even for Indians, who are small of stature, their cramped quarters make travel difficult—particularly when extra passengers sit on boards spanning the aisles or stand wedged into the driver's compartment.

Once off the main roads, the buses cover about fifteen miles in an hour, stopping frequently to pick up passengers (often whole families at a time). Most of the women are barefooted and carry babies on their backs. The men, usually in shoddy dark wool suits, help with the baggage, deposit their *machetes* just inside the door, and force their way into the already packed aisle to stand for the duration of the bone-wracking journey. With nearly every passenger comes a cargo of something destined for market. Huge, unwieldy bundles of fruits, vegetables, grain, and other marketable items are hoisted onto the shoulders of the driver's assistant, who struggles up the metal ladder welded to the vehicle's rear and dumps each load onto the roof with a resounding thump that rocks the bus. Itinerant photographers have little choice in their mode of travel; they must go along with everybody else, their tripods, cameras, backdrops, photo supplies, and personal effects riding on top of the bus with livestock and garden produce.

Public transportation in Guatemala is reasonably inexpensive. The buses are slow, rigorous, and often unpredictable, but drivers try to keep to a loose schedule. Though the greater percentage of Indians walk to market and many other itinerant merchants travel the mountain trails on foot, photographers rely almost exclusively on the complicated network of buses that connects major towns with all but the most isolated villages.

Trucks and buses headed for remote towns and villages leave well before daybreak in order to arrive in time for the morning market. Their jagged, top-heavy contours are silhouetted against the horizon's eerie predawn light as they top steep ridges and go roaring down inclines, trailing clouds of oily smoke and splitting the country quiet with popping staccato blasts from hot exhausts. In the first fleeting rays of sunshine drivers race long shadows cast by their vehicles against the cut banks of zigzagging mountain roads. Passengers talk animatedly between breakfast snacks, doze, shiver in the raw chill of morning, or doggedly endure the sweltering heat. The lumbering buses jolt and sway, climbing and descending precipitous switchbacks that twist like serpents along mountain heights of breathtaking beauty. Occupants brace themselves for hairpin curves and settle back in their seats on the straightaways. With every lurch forward, clattering gears clash, grind, and whine as antiquated motors strain to keep from stalling. The close interiors become stuffy as a conglomeration of suffocating odors permeate their stagnant space. People nod in restless sleep and finally sink into a kind of numbed lethargy. The sullen monotony is broken only by the birdman's chirping parakeets swaying overhead in cloth-covered cages.

At a major fair photographers will usually set up their equipment a day or two in advance of the saint's day, called by them *el dia mas alegre* (the most festive day). This is done to make themselves familiar to prospective patrons, even though they expect little business before the scheduled festivities. The Indians who have also arrived early get used to their presence, which helps them to overcome their shyness when it comes time to have their pictures taken.

Itinerant photographers have long been assigned their particular areas—beside a prominent water fountain, at one corner of a public square, close to where buses disgorge passengers, or along the sidewalk fronting a row of buildings leading from the main plaza to the market site. If a celebration is held away from the center of town they line up along the roadside leading to the fairgrounds. Their only requirements seem to be that they be easily seen by people coming and going and that they have enough room to work. From one to a dozen photographers may unfurl their painted backdrops and set up business during any given fair.

Fairs in the Guatemalan highlands commence with a flurry of early morning activity as barren plazas burgeon into riotous color. Poles are lashed together to form market stalls, and photographers set up soon after sunrise in order to catch the first light and the few individuals who want their pictures taken then and there. These early customers are often the ones who have quickly sold their merchandise and are returning home to work their fields. Ordinarily, business for photographers begins to pick up in mid-morning and is heaviest toward mid-afternoon.

Patience as practiced by itinerants achieves a kind of stubborn virtue. They often must wait long hours between sittings as uninterested Indians scurry to and from the marketplace. Lean days are typical before an annual fair has really gotten underway. During such slack times photographers read, talk among themselves, or just stand around waiting for clients. Some relax astride their wooden horses. If the weather is chilly they warm themselves with cups of piping hot *atole*, a traditional drink of water thickened with cornstarch and sometimes flavored with sweet chocolate or vanilla. They converse softly about everything except how little work they have. If asked how business is they say that, although it is quiet at the moment, the following day will be a big one. Years of experience have taught itinerant photographers the psychology that impels the Indian to leave his most important transactions until near the end of a fair.

On bad days an itinerant may take fewer than half a dozen photographs, but on busy days his eternal optimism is vindicated. He may have dozens of sittings, working steadily from early morning until dusk. There are accounts (perhaps exaggerated) of photographers making a hundred or more pictures in a single day.

Itinerants are vigilant about staying on the job. Even one bent on a drinking spree will usually manage to put in an appearance for at least part of the day before he disappears into the nearest *cantina*. Recesses are taken only when necessary, and then preferably when a colleague can mind the business so the photographer can be summoned in case a customer appears. If a stall is left untended, the owner covers his camera with a cloth or with his coat or sets it aside, leaving his empty tripod standing in front of the backdrop as an indication that he will return soon. When business is booming the itinerant buys food from passing vendors, gulps soft drinks, and stays with his machine. He periodically adjusts the canvas flaps joined to his backdrop to control the sunlight, and finally pins them back altogether to catch the last flicker of fading light. He will work until there is no hope of making a decent photograph.

When the workday is over the photographer packs up, rolls his backdrop, and puts away all his accessories. He sometimes pays a boy or an old man a few cents to carry everything to a prearranged storage place. It is not safe to leave things unattended after dark, partly because of wind and weather but chiefly because drunken revelers may stumble over them. There is a great deal of drunkenness at fairs; both Indians and *ladinos* drink copiously to celebrate or give vent to pent-up emotions.

After every fair buses are again filled beyond any respect for legal capacity; seats are doubled up with passengers and the narrow aisles are packed with exhausted merchants and drunken Indians—often the very people who only a few hours before had sat for formal portraits. When the itinerant photographers leave it is probable that no more pictures will be made in that village until the next festival.

Regular market days, especially those that fall in the middle of the week, prove to be poor pickings for itinerant photographers. Unless there is a special celebration it is quite unusual for one to show up at all. If a photographer does appear he is more than likely based locally or an itinerant on his way to a fair in some other region, stopping off between buses in hopes of earning a little extra money. Local photographers seldom burden themselves with props or painted backdrops, but simply use a plain cloth casually draped against a wall. Typically an itinerant finds that by early afternoon, when the market crowds have thinned to stragglers and sensible merchants have already packed up and gone home, he may have had only two or three sittings—barely enough to show a profit after bus fare and cost of materials. However, for many itinerants even a slim profit can make the difference in providing for family necessities. Buses usually stand parked in rows while drivers and their helpers call out destinations and hustle people aboard. Market-weary passengers peer drowsily out of half-opened windows as they munch peanuts or lick two-penny popsicles. Their cache of purchases and their untraded wares are piled about them as they wait for the bus to fill so they can begin their journey homeward. By mid-afternoon a less-than-dedicated itinerant will catch the next bus out, perhaps having first done some needed shopping or visiting to justify his excursion. A more persistent colleague may know that the probability of further work is unlikely but still be reluctant to leave until the final minute. As soon as he sees the last bus about to depart for his village, he hurriedly collects his camera gear and rushes to get aboard.

There is little need for itinerant photographers to advertise. If a photograph is wanted, the prospective client simply waits for a fair; itinerants are sure to show up. However, a few enterprising photographers carry printed business cards and occasionally promote their establishments with cheap illustrated calendars. Generally, though, advertising is by word of mouth or confined to the exhibition of examples featuring a variety of poses and sizes (to demonstrate the photographer's range and capability), mounted on boards in batches of a dozen or more and framed under glass. These display boards are usually hinged together in units of three or four and hung vertically from awning poles so that prospective customers can study them. Such displays are always popular. They attract crowds of shy girls and curious young men who search among the photographs for familiar faces from previous fairs and flirtatiously goad each other into having pictures taken. Even on a slow day these pictorial panels attract passers-by who contemplate the collected images before moving on to attend to the real business of their day. Fascinated children amuse themselves for hours in this manner, slowly moving from one photographer's booth to another, cherishing the faint hope that they, too, might be photographed before the fair ends.

Photographers' props are fairly standardized. Their principal requirements are that they be eye-catching, useful, and portable. Each photographer has at least one folding chair, more than likely painted a bright color. This is commonly used for both single and group portraits, for setting toddlers on, for storing bundles while a client poses, or, when business is slack, for the photographer himself to rest upon. Each set also features a bunch of travel-weary plastic flowers stuck into a cheap jug, tin can, or old thermos bottle nailed to a flimsy little stand. Oddly, this still life seems present more for tradition than for any other purpose, for it is seldom included in the sittings. Sometimes a replica of one of these stands or tables appears, complete with its bouquet of flowers, as part of a painted backdrop.

Much more popular are the *caballitos* (the sprightly painted wooden horses) and their cousins, the boldly striped zebras, which are standard equipment for most itinerant photographers. These comical little animals are sometimes delicately carved, and nearly all are decorated with saddles and other gaily colored equestrian trappings. A few are even polka-dotted in lurid colors or patterned with fantastic flowers that appeal immensely to children. The appeal, however, is purely visual, for young children usually scream with terror at finding themselves suddenly mounted astride such strange creatures. *Caballitos* cost around $45.00 to have made and are a major investment for photographers. In Guatemala City a relative of one of the itinerants specializes in carving these miniature horses and supplies most of the present-day market. Lighter models are constructed of *papier maché*, heavily gessoed and shellacked for durability. Some of the larger horses have detachable heads; this makes them easier to transport and store. For travel these quaint little beasts are carefully swaddled in sackcloth or canvas and lashed securely, sometimes with a folding chair alongside for added protection.

When the horse is trotted out there is usually an accompanying ensemble consisting of a Mexican-style *sombrero*, a cartridge belt with leather holsters, and a pair of wooden six-guns to complete the illusion. It is a seductive combination for exuberant young men who wish to show off in front of the camera. It lures older men as well, especially those who have imbibed enough of a fiery cane liquor called *aguardiente* to remind them of cowboy movies or their own youthful ranching days. The men behind the cameras seem unperturbed by displays of drunken behavior; they manage these clients as effectively as they do frightened and howling children.

Mirrors are among the smallest and most useful articles in the itinerant photographer's meager pack, for they enable subjects to scrutinize themselves while making last-minute preparations for the sitting. They are attached to the sides of cameras or suspended from awning poles. Sometimes a garish plastic comb can be found floating in the bucket of water used for rinsing prints. Women and young girls busy themselves in front of the silvered glass as though primping for a party, combing and rebraiding their hair, arranging beautifully embroidered *huipiles* to hang just so over arms and shoulders, posing with the help of friends or family, and joking with the covey of giggling girls who have accompanied them. Immediately upon taking a pose, however, each girl's face changes suddenly to an expression of seriousness as an Indian stoicism exerts itself. The camera's magic is already beginning to work. Some of the men, too, stoop to peer into mirrors as they comb their glossy hair and practice sober expressions. Many furtively check their reflections in tiny pocket mirrors, cupping them in calloused hands held at waist level. They preen until pleased with their appearance, then slip the round glass into a shirt pocket and take their rigid stance against the painted backdrop.

The pungent smell of shoe polish and shouts of "*Lustre?*" are always associated with itinerant photographers during fairs; boisterous and persistent shoeshine boys stay in close proximity with their portable kits ready to fight for the business of clients who want their shoes touched up before having pictures taken.

A dark coat (usually the photographer's own) and a black clip-on necktie are available if patrons want formal portraits. After a quick consultation the photographer helps his customer into the coat, adjusts the tie, then seats him in a dignified pose, usually in front of a wall or a plain dark cloth. The transformation of a country-costumed Indian by the mere addition of an ordinary suit coat and tie can be dramatic.

Much indigenous charm is lost from the portraits because Indians prefer formal poses. Men usually remove their hats, causing their features to take on an entire change of character. Women who come to market wearing fantastic headdresses or bearing colorful bundles on their heads insist upon taking them off before stepping in front of a camera. Also, they submit to the latest fashion by covering their native blouses with gaudy factory-made sweaters. In such cases, the photographic results are less exciting than the exotic visions that first presented themselves to the photographer. Once in a while customers supply their own props, requesting to be photographed with a portable radio, a newly purchased kettle, or some other cherished object to be commemorated. It is not unusual for people to be photographed with chickens, turkeys, or even piglets in their arms.

The box-type cameras used by itinerants are home-manufactured from the dismantled parts of old cameras. They are surprisingly similar, not only throughout Guatemala but in such far-off places as Peru, Italy, Spain, and India, where itinerant and park photographers continue to ply their trade. The overall design has changed very little for more than half a century. In fact, many of the cameras being used today have already seen service for several decades. Even when new ones are constructed, the same time-proven pattern is followed closely. One important clue to the similarity lies in the fact that these photographers do not have a conventional laboratory at their disposal, and must carry their laboratories with them. This is managed by what is in effect a portable darkroom, or, as they call it, a *mini-laboratorio*: small trays for chemicals, a holder for photographic paper, and a lightproof sleeve through which an arm can be inserted for manipulation during the developing process.

The overall dimensions of the cameras average twelve inches high, ten inches wide, and sixteen inches long. Most of the boxes' exteriors are covered with treated black cloth, their seams and edges sealed with strips of soft metal; some are made of varnished or brightly painted wood. With small variations, most cameras possess the following similar features: The solid underside has an embedded screw mount that allows the camera to be attached to a plain but sturdy wooden tripod, adjusted by telescoping or changing the angle of the legs. On the camera's front is a hinged door that, when opened, reveals the mechanical parts. A movable L-shaped attachment that fits into a slot beneath this opened door serves to position the wet paper negative in front of the lens while the image is rephotographed to obtain a positive print. A simple close-up lens is placed over the ordinary lens for this procedure.

The lens, the shutter, and the bellows are affixed to metal runners that permit the entire unit to extend or retract for focusing. This assembly is nearly always taken from large roll-film cameras dating from the 1920s and 1930s. These obsolete machines, so out of fashion today except among collectors, are available inexpensively and can, with a minimum investment, be adapted to suit the needs of itinerant photographers. Some of the mechanisms remain in good condition and possess fair optical quality, but it is more likely that they have been reduced to bandaged bellows, scratched lenses, and faulty shutters. A correct exposure depends not only upon the photographer's ability to judge his light but also upon good reflex timing as his fingers release the shutter cord. A removable piece of ground glass replaces the old camera's original back and the itinerant's homemade box becomes, in effect, a view camera.

Developing is done within the camera. The photographer's arm fits into the lightproof sleeve, which allows for positioning and developing the negative and its print. Small trays of developer and fixer are placed inside the back section of the *mini-laboratorio* along with a box containing precut photographic paper. Because paper negatives are used rather than film emulsion there is no need for more than one developing solution.

Prints are washed in a bucket conveniently placed beneath the tripod. Photographs made in this manner are jokingly referred to by itinerants as *fotos cubitosos,* or "bucket photos," to distinguish them from studio work. It is not unusual for a single pail of water to wash the entire day's output. Chickens drink from it, people rinse their hands in it, and small children peer into its polluted depths to watch their reflections as they stir the surface with grimy fingers. The wadded end of a soiled cloth is wedged into the fork of a tripod leg, where it hangs limply to serve as a hand towel to wipe off wet photographs. This casualness ensures that all prints are tainted by chemicals and therefore rendered impermanent. Indeed, some start to yellow before the fair is over. Small squares of newsprint serve as absorbent folders for newly washed photographs. Each day's supply is strung together with snippets of cord or safety-pinned by one corner to form a sheaf, which is attached to some handy part of the camera or its tripod.

Photographers usually install viewing windows of deep red glass or plastic in the sides of their machines. Discarded automobile brake-light covers are frequently adapted to this purpose. Such an innovation makes possible development by inspection, a very useful technique when one is using an unreliable shutter and when the solutions are of unknown temperature and questionable freshness. These windows are kept covered when not in use. In some instances an extra door is cut into the side of the box, and on virtually all cameras the top panel is hinged to open like a chest. This permits ready access for cleaning and makes the inside space usable for storage of materials when traveling. Interiors are often lined with oilcloth to facilitate the cleaning of spilled chemical solutions. To this basic camera many practical extras can be added, such as sturdy metal handles and simple gunsight viewing devices. Home-made sun shades are occasionally employed, but it is more typical for a photographer to use his hat to shade the lens.

From time to time one sees tiny brushes and bottles of retouching dye fitted into snug little holders on the side of a camera. As the Indians are dark-skinned, these dyes are discreetly used to give a lighter skin tone on the final print. Photographers seem to have no doubts that this is what their customers want, but as a result their images often have strangely washed-out, characterless faces.

A typical sitting takes place in the following manner: The photographer will inquire first whether his customer wants a closeup of head and shoulders (a *medio cuerpo*, or half body) against a plain background or a full portrait using part or all of a painted backdrop. The former is for use on official papers and the latter is usually a memento. The memento-type picture frequently includes more than one person. (The price remains the same whether for an individual or an entire family.) The photographer places his customer in the desired position, moves his tripod to an approximate distance, and opens the small door at the rear of his camera so that he can focus an image on the ground glass inside. The subject is often repositioned several times at this point. When satisfied, the photographer instructs his subject not to move. He closes the shutter and fastens the door on the back of his camera, then thrusts his arm into the light-tight sleeve. The inside of the camera is now totally dark. With one hand the photographer removes the ground glass, manipulates a piece of photo paper from its storage compartment inside his *mini-laboratorio*, and places it into position behind the lens. When this is done he withdraws his arm from the sleeve and stands poised with the shutter cord held between his thumb and forefinger. He again advises his client not to move ("*No te muevas . . . No te muevas!*"), to close his mouth ("*Cerra la boca*"), and to look directly into the camera. He then takes off his hat, shades the lens with it, and quickly releases the shutter.

The paper negative is now exposed and ready to be developed, but the customer is cautioned to hold his pose until the photographer is quite sure the picture is satisfactory. (Often a photograph has to be retaken; one of the group, usually a child, may have disrupted the pose, fairgoers may have walked between camera and subject or accidentally kicked the tripod, or the paper may have become dislodged within the camera.) The photographer reaches into the sleeve, removes the paper negative, and dips it into the small tray of developer. The paper is agitated in this solution for about a minute and then placed in the hypo. None of this is apparent from the outside, so customers seldom have any idea as to what is taking place. For unsophisticated clients the magic of photography is considerably enhanced by these obscure machinations.

After the negative has been in the hypo for a few seconds the camera's door is opened and the negative is inspected. If satisfied, the photographer tells his customer to come back for the print in fifteen or twenty minutes. More often than not Indians stay to watch the mysterious process, generally with quiet reserve but sometimes nudging and exclaiming to each other as they recognize their images on the submerged bits of paper.

When the negative is fixed it is briefly washed and dried with a cloth. At this point, if the photographer feels it is necessary, skin tones are tinted. The negative is then positioned in front of the lens by means of the L-shaped device fitted onto the front of the camera. The shutter is again opened, and the photographer fits his simple close-up lens over the ordinary lens and readjusts both lens and negative to obtain a sharply focused image of the correct size on the ground glass. When this has been done the shutter is closed, the exposure is made, and the print is developed. If two or more small or medium-sized prints are desired, the paper is shifted after each exposure and methodically exposed by halves or quarters.

Payment is not made until photographs are delivered. The itinerant dips into the pail of water and fishes about with his fingers until he selects the proper print, which he lifts out dripping and carefully dries. The limp photo is trimmed with scissors and neatly placed into a folded sheet of blank newsprint, then handed (with a flourish if the subject happens to be a pretty girl) to the waiting customer. At that point a slightly secretive, almost ritualistic transaction takes place involving the exchange of coins for pictures. The person photographed quickly walks some distance away before inspecting his or her likeness. Even when people are disappointed with the results, photographs are seldom rejected. If a customer is not present when his picture is finished it is left in the bucket until called for. Naturally there are exceptions to this routine. For example, when a photographer is working with many subjects, as in the case of military recruitment, a system is worked out so that photographs are made in groups on an organized basis and payment is sometimes received in advance.

As primitive paintings, the elaborate scenes used as photographic backdrops are a genre unto themselves. Generally painted in glaring colors on stitched-together pieces of heavy canvas, they measure six to eight feet square and are designed to hang tautly stretched from horizontal poles. These curiously painted backdrops are usually called *paisajes*, or landscapes. Other names are *telon*, which literally means "large cloth," or *fondo*, meaning "background" or "curtain" (more specifically, "theatrical curtain"). These terms are seldom used, however; since most backgrounds depict landscapes or cityscapes, itinerants commonly speak of all backdrops as *paisajes*. They are, with the possible exception of his camera, the most expensive single item in the itinerant photographer's outfit.

During work sessions practically all painted backgrounds are shaded by plain white awnings called *velas* and by wings cut from the same material. Most of the day these appendages are used to shield both backdrops and customers from direct sunlight, but by late afternoon they can be angled to reflect the fading light or rolled up altogether. They also give an intimate boothlike appearance to each itinerant's working space.

The *paisajes* are imaginatively conceived and executed, although, as is true of much primitive painting, their composition often borders on the chaotic. The artists who are commissioned to paint them employ a crude perspective that delights the eye as it strives for added dimensions. Architectural motifs are sometimes boldly outlined in black, giving the whole a stark illustrative quality reminiscent of early hand-colored woodprints.

Backdrops fall roughly into four categories. Probably the most popular are those showing important landmarks such as churches, national shrines (a prime example being detailed representations of Guatemala's National Palace), or panoramic park scenes. Related, but different in mood, are contemporary metropolitan scenes with towering buildings, business signs, and crowded thoroughfares. One fascinating example, probably inspired by a picture postcard, portrays a cityscape of ultramodern buildings identified by the caption "San Paulo, Brasil." Another, equally intriguing, features the artist's vision of Peru's bustling capital and is labeled "Avenida 'Wilson', Lima, Peru, America del Sur." It is not unusual for a rural Indian family to choose an urban scene, perhaps because it suggests that they have actually journeyed to such a metropolis. Although the name of the city is often plainly spelled out on a design, Indians are rarely aware that they have chosen to be photographed in a foreign setting.

Another type of backdrop depicts fantasy scenes with storybook castles, arched stone bridges, flowing fountains, angels, swans gliding on placid lakes, and, not infrequently, Guatemala's national emblem, the quetzal bird, in flight across a highly romantic landscape. At least one photographer's *paisaje* is made from pictorially printed cloth—two yardage lengths of a pastoral scene sewn together and supplemented with artistic retouching and a romantic slogan.

There is also a broad range of memento-type backgrounds. These introduce stylized drapery, flower- or vine-wreathed columns, and flying banners inscribed with sentiments ranging from the simple "*Recuerdo*" (remembrance) or "*Recuerdo inovidable*" (unforgettable remembrance) to the more elaborate "*Recuerdos de hoy y siempre. Si te alejas acuerdate de mi*" (Memories of today and always. If you go away, remember me). Common also to these designs are lavish floral arrangements, the symbolic quetzal roosting on a pedestal, and fluttering doves holding messages in their beaks. A very popular background from Huehuetenango is inscribed "*El Paraiso de mis Recuerdos*" (the paradise of my memories).

Not all backdrops are ornately decorated. On regular market days, if a photographer shows up at all, he more than likely brings only a large square of dyed cloth, which he suspends like a curtain from a strand of rope stretched between two nails or wooden pegs driven into an adobe wall. This material can be black, purple, pink, or any color that provides a suitable contrast for the person photographed against it. Sometimes the cloth is gathered and looped into a massive knot or simply pushed aside when not in use. In some cases the photographer dispenses with the backdrop altogether and shoots his pictures directly against the light-colored, smooth surface of a wall.

From time to time one encounters backdrops of such inferior quality that one must assume they were home-painted by inexperienced hands to save the cost of having them done by a professional. These are acceptable for identification or everyday-type photographs, but they lack style and excite little interest among *fiesta*-goers. It usually follows that the photographers who have crude and poorly painted backdrops are either the beginners or the ones who are most careless in their craft.

It costs anywhere from twenty to ninety dollars to have a backdrop painted by the men (usually journeyman sign painters) who take on such odd assignments. Their prices depend upon the artist's reputation, the kind of picture wanted, and the amount of time or planning required. A particularly complicated design—for instance, a metropolitan scene with skyscrapers, neon signs, lots of people, automobiles, and airplanes—could very well cost the maximum figure. Ordinarily, prices are agreed upon beforehand and the finished product is promised for delivery within two or three weeks.

According to some photographers, a substantial number of older *paisajes* originated in Mexico and were sold to Guatemalans when Mexico's itinerant tradition gradually gave way to other forms of photography. These represent typical Mexican landmarks such as religious shrines and cityscapes like those of Tapachula or Mexico City's *Zocalo* with its splendid colonial cathedral.

The colorful *paisajes* used by Guatemalan photographers represent a specialized form of folk art solely dependent upon the itinerant tradition. When the demand for this kind of photography is gone, the backdrops will soon disappear as they already have in other parts of the world.

A particularly skillful painter of photographic backgrounds lives in the vicinity of Quezaltenango and signs his canvases "Herman Montalgo, Totonicapán." *Paisajes* tend to have certain similarities, but this man's lush style is immediately recognizable because of his provocative colors and careful attention to composition and detail. Orlando Enrique Herrera, an artist from Huehuetenango who has a peculiarly florid style, also specializes in backdrops. His prices average about fifty dollars. Another painter of decorative and well-executed backdrops is Celestino Ciriaco Perez, a well-known itinerant photographer who works out of a studio in Escuintla. He has a good reputation as an artist, and creates imaginative designs not only for himself and his father Geronimo but for many of his colleagues.

Although backdrops are painted in bright colors, photographs are almost always made in black and white. Considering that most scenes are carefully designed to evoke a fantasy environment, they are used quite carelessly. More often than not a rope is strung across the middle of a glorious landscape and on it the dark curtain used for plain backgrounds is hung. This rope serves as a catchall for casually draped jackets, bags, and other odds and ends, which block out much of the painted scene. If the curtain happens to have been pulled across the lower half of a *paisaje* for one sitting it is often not drawn back for the next. Even when a scene of strict formality is desired, clients are seldom positioned in the obvious "right place" and photographers tend to give the backdrop little thought when composing their pictures. The grass-bare earth or paving stones in front of an itinerant's stall are never swept, so by the end of the day all kinds of litter is scattered about, and it usually ends up as part of the picture. Also immortalized are bottles of developing solution, the buckets used for washing prints, and miscellaneous bundles laid aside by customers. Neither the photographer nor the person photographed seem bothered by these details. For eyes accustomed to the pristine fantasy worlds created by American and European fashion magazines this is difficult to accept.

When not in use, the canvas backdrops are wound tightly about their slender poles, tied, and stored until the next round of fairs. When in transit they are roped with the rest of the photographer's paraphernalia to the luggage rack on top of the bus. They are quite durable, but many backdrops show signs of wear and tear from years of hard use. Weathering and constant travel take their toll. It is not uncommon to find ripped backdrops stitched together and patched over and over again. Whole areas of faded paint are sometimes touched up.

The average life of a backdrop is probably between ten and fifteen years. Some last longer and can still be seen at fairs in various stages of disintegration. Before backdrops are retired they are often passed on at low prices to apprentices. They are also lent back and forth, which accounts for some backdrops showing up at divers times and places with different photographers. An itinerant may take a favorite backdrop to a certain fair because he had good luck with it during a previous visit. Families who own several backdrops are considered fortunate because they can select those they feel are best suited for particular celebrations.

Photographers can recount the full histories of many *paisajes*—their successive owners; where, when, and by whom they were painted; and numerous incidents associated with their use over the years. For instance, several years ago an itinerant made the rounds of fairs with a backdrop featuring a fierce-looking Bengal tiger. It was a beautifully painted canvas but not as popular as the photographer had hoped it might be. It was retired when he realized that the reason it failed to attract customers was that children and timid Indians were genuinely frightened of the beast's menacing appearance.

Indians from the Guatemalan highlands are noted for their shyness and reserve. Itinerant photographers, many of them Indians themselves who have become urbanized, maintain a sympathetic understanding of these characteristics and treat their clients accordingly. Years of experience plus an intuitive knowledge of their countrymen's habits enable them to deal effectively with the multifaceted Indian psychology.

Unlike roving vendors or clothing merchants, photographers do not resort to blatant hucksterism to solicit business. Quite the opposite is true; their approach is one of gentle persuasion. They are adept at luring customers into the shade of their awnings and in front of their cameras. They scorn hard-sell techniques, and seem totally indifferent when prospective clients wander off to another photographer's booth or decide to have no photograph taken at all.

If a fairgoer slows his walk in passing, a photographer may call out softly "*Quiere un foto?*" If he detects any interest he swings his arm in a broad sweeping motion toward his stall and says "*Pase adelante*" to invite him in, or he merely points to his sample board. If the prospective customer responds by stopping to inspect the mounted photographs, the two engage in a low-voiced, almost whispered conversation to determine whether there is serious interest in having a picture taken. If not, the photographer does little to encourage or cajole and returns to the shade of his awning to await another prospect. On the other hand, if price has been discussed, the type of photograph decided upon, and an agreement reached, the photographer immediately becomes very businesslike. He assumes an air of gentle but firm authority and proceeds with the sitting.

Having a picture taken is no frivolous matter for shy Guatemalan Indians; it is attended with solemnity and much preparation. So at this point the magic begins. Features suddenly take on an unusually sober expression. The body straightens to form a rigid pose, and the subject gradually retreats into himself until he achieves an almost trancelike immobility. It is all very serious and mystical.

The superstition that has persisted among uninformed peoples since the invention of photography still exists in the Guatemalan highlands. It is sincerely believed by many Indians that a person's soul is captured in a photographic image. Whoever possesses that picture can, if so desired, use it to work evil against the individual photographed. In one dramatic instance a family with an ailing child was sitting for a group portrait. The father, perceiving that they were also about to be photographed by an outsider, requested that only the itinerant's camera be used because his dangerously ill baby might not have the strength to resist the power of another camera. He had overcome enough of his fear to accept having a portrait made (perhaps the last memento of his sick child), yet he dared not risk the threat of a stranger's camera.

Only a very small percentage of those who pass a photographer's booth have their pictures taken. Those fairgoers who are most traditional in costume and manner consult photographers far less often than do townsfolk, for whom the photograph plays a more familiar role in daily life. This is partly because Indians in *traje* (indigenous dress) have less money to spend on such vanities. It is also due to their underlying fear and apprehension at being photographed. However, once the decision has been made, Indians accept it with a kind of fatalistic resignation and sit composed and dignified until the ordeal is behind them.

If a photograph is necessary for an identification card, the subject gets it over with as quickly as possible. By contrast, a family portrait sitting might involve much discussion and shopping around before a particular photographer is decided upon (generally because he has a backdrop which appeals to them). It is also a psychologically persuasive inducement if an itinerant appears busier than his colleagues. Sometimes, undecided clients will spend hours trekking back and forth, studying the posted boards and talking to photographers in an effort to come to a decision while at the same time prolonging their choice until the final moment. A bit of urging or flirtatious banter will help to convince a pretty girl and her wavering companions. Boisterous drunks and swaggering young men dare each other until one finally dons a *sombrero* and poses manfully with a brace of wooden pistols. Timid couples, perhaps only recently married, often pose together for a photographic memento.

Once a person is committed to having a picture taken, the photographer nods to confirm the agreement and by a series of skillful maneuvers hurriedly guides his client to a suitable place in front of the camera. He is careful to betray no eagerness, and his behavior appears considerate beyond politeness as he repositions his tripod and focuses his lens until an appropriate pose is struck. To put his customer at ease, he may say a few words in Quiché or Mam, depending on the linguistic area and his own knowledge of the dialect.

A photographer does not expect an Indian to smile on such a solemn occasion, nor would he ask him to; he might, instead, if confronted by a gaping mouth, order it closed. A photographer seldom touches his client, either; if so it is done ever so gently, merely to suggest or direct, perhaps to arrange a detail of hair or clothing or the angle of a face, and usually with the tips of his fingers only. The manner is firm but the touch is soft. When working with scared or restless children some itinerants employ squeaking or mechanical toys to gain the child's attention. More often they clap their hands together, emit sharp whistles, or wave their hats in soaring arcs to coax children into looking in the right direction.

Indians who are totally unfamiliar with the photographic process seldom know when their pictures have been taken, and often walk away while the itinerant is still adjusting his lens. Others stand frozen in the same position long after an exposure has been made and will not move until the photographer signals them to. Indian girls pose uneasily for a few seconds, then, clued by the sound of the shutter's click, immediately dash out of camera range.

If asked to, an Indian woman will sometimes share the first viewing of her photograph with bystanders. After a brief scrutiny and some jocular comments, she will tuck the picture into her bosom and go about her affairs. Men who have worked the soil for the money they are spending on this dubious luxury hold photographs in their work-toughened hands for a careful look, then tenderly consign them to the tiny woven bags containing coins and other valuables that are carried around their necks. Sometimes whole families will huddle together to appraise their group image, staring incredulously or laughing at the camera's uncompromising treatment of their features.

There is always a crowd around a busy photographer's booth. Old and young move in close to watch the itinerant work, marveling and exclaiming when they see themselves or their friends on paper submerged in a bucket of water. Customers are not always pleased with what they see, but photographs are seldom rejected and payment is rarely withheld. Nor is there any pressure on the part of itinerants to sell additional copies, a practice commonly employed by studio photographers. Itinerants know their market, and few have thoughts of exceeding it.

Chichicastenango is undoubtedly the most famous regional market center in Guatemala. Tourists from all over the world go there to shop and observe the primitive religious rites. Visiting Indians fire off powerful homemade skyrockets to petition the heavens and burn *copal* on the worn stone steps leading into the church. The town, located in the heart of an agricultural district, has served for centuries as a gathering place for Indians who combine marketing with religious pilgrimages. At Christmas,

Easter, and other holidays thousands of natives wearing exceptionally colorful costumes pour in from the surrounding villages. They shop, celebrate, and pray in the historic sixteenth-century church and the stark white El Calvario Chapel, which face each other at opposite ends of the plaza. Many celebrants accentuate their happiness or drown their sorrows with *aguardiente*, which by late afternoon litters the streets with Indians in their last stages of inebriation.

Although Chichicastenango has become a tourist stopover, the regular Thursday and Sunday markets have retained much of their indigenous flavor. Nonetheless, itinerant photographers insist that it is only a moderately good town for their type of work. They prefer to visit during the special festivals (particularly the fair in honor of the town's patron saint, the Apóstol Santo Tomás, in mid-December), when they are reasonably sure of earning good wages.

Chichicastenango is also a military conscription center. The government requires that eligible males over the age of eighteen must serve two years in the army. On specified dates potential inductees line up in close formation and stand for hours outside a barracks building to await registration. Since each one must be photographed, it is always a profitable outing for those lucky itinerants who manage to be present. If the claims are true that itinerants occasionally exceed a hundred photographs in a single day, it would have to be under circumstances similar to these. When the session begins a mob of new recruits crowds around the itinerant's stall. In such cases photographers nearly always work with assistants, most often sons or nephews who are learning the trade. They prefer shooting pictures in an "assembly line" series so a group of negatives can be processed together. One takes photographs and develops the negatives while the other makes final prints with a second camera. Payment is made in advance. One by one the men are guided awkwardly to a stool in front of the camera. Hats are always removed for identification photographs, and clients sit, rigid and ill at ease, staring straight into the camera's lens. As quickly as one group is processed another takes its place.

After the itinerant has completed a series of identification photographs, he holds them up to be claimed. He could not possibly match up so many similar faces and poses. At this point there is always confusion as country Indians—unaccustomed to scrutinizing their features, even as reflections in mirrors—try to make their selections. Many of them simply cannot recognize their own images. They stare at the photographs, then at one another. By now, they are again wearing hats, so even their companions have difficulty connecting the actual persons with the grim visages peering back from tiny squares of paper. Often, in the midst of such commotions, a photographer is forced to interrupt his work and intervene. He goes from one Indian to another, lifting each man's hat and, with the aid of the rambunctious crowd, matching faces to his fistful of unclaimed photographs. When (after much laughing and wrangling) the pictures are sorted out and given to their respective owners, many still cannot accept that they have received the proper photographs and go on staring in disbelief at the strange images. This is probably less a reflection on the itinerant's ability as a photographer than it is on the Indian's inability to visualize himself as a disembodied entity. Such fast-paced projects can last all day, and photographers stay on the job until all recruits have been recorded. This kind of work can be a bonanza for itinerants, but at the end of the long day they wearily admit that they have earned every penny.

In the larger cities of Guatemala a different kind of itinerant, the park or street photographer, is generally found on Sundays and holidays in public parks. On weekdays they sometimes take their cameras to prominent churches and historical sites to be on hand when out-of-town visitors are most likely to appear. Some of them travel to fairs, but most are content to stay at their favorite spots in town.

On Sundays, Guatemala City's Parque Aurora is the principal attraction for thousands of the city's populace. It is a broad, tree-filled area with a zoo and numerous small concessions. Stalls selling soft drinks and regional foods line the sidewalks leading into the park. The cool, pleasant surroundings make it an excellent place for picnicking, courting, or just relaxing. It is also a traditional gathering place for photographers. Every Sunday a score or more of the regulars take their cameras to an assigned place just inside the park's entrance gate, where they set up their tripods and wait for business. Painted backdrops are not permitted inside the park, but on a dusty triangular plot across the street from the entrance where this rule does not apply one can usually find two or three photographers working with scenic backdrops. Business is slow during the morning hours, but photographers set up their equipment and spend the time joking and chatting among themselves. Some haul out wooden horses and other trappings from a storage building located nearby on the grounds. The rental for this handy arrangement is split several ways, and thus costs each participant only a few cents a month.

Activity picks up around noon, and by mid-afternoon the park is swarming with people who promenade its tree-lined walkways and occasionally stop to pose for photographs. Men with Polaroids wander among the crowds, which are chiefly made up of families on outings with their children, young men alone or in pairs searching for feminine companionship, and visitors from the country who spend much of their time observing the caged animals. The photographers' best prospects are the *criadas*, the servants of well-to-do and middle-class *ladino* families. These young women usually do not make their appearance until after three o'clock, when the midday meal is over and they are at liberty to leave. Those who are country girls use these weekly outings to dress in their native costumes and their showiest jewelry, presumedly to attract the attention of visiting males from the villages of their home area. They parade the park in chattering groups and are addicted to having their pictures taken for sending home or giving to admirers. The photographers eagerly await them, not only for the business they bring but also for their high spirits. The days when *criadas* have just been paid their monthly wages are grand events for them and for the photographers.

The park teems with visitors throughout the early afternoon; then, quite suddenly, as though by prearrangement, the crowds disperse and all activity shifts to the bustling food stalls and sidewalk vendors stationed near the main entrance gates. By dusk the photographers have packed up and gone home and there are only a few straggling promenaders left waiting for buses into the center of town.

Itinerant photographers speak almost reverently of *La Época de la Cedula* (the epoch of the identity card), a three-month period in 1970 and 1971 when every citizen and resident over the age of eighteen was required to register and be photographed for the *cedula*, a pocket-sized identity card without which a person cannot vote, take certain jobs, or do much of anything official. This was decreed by the new government as, so some maintain, a means of political control. (According to older photographers this had happened once before within their memory, sometime during the 1930s.) Word went out to even the remotest mountain and jungle villages, and Indians began coming to the market sites where itinerant photographers gathered. Long lines formed and many people waited for hours to have pictures taken. It was a golden time for itinerant photographers. They were on the road day and night, dividing up territories and working frantically to harvest the bonanza. As one intinerant recalls, "Photographers came out of the walls. Everybody with a camera was working."

Photographers still speak of this period as the great time in their working lives. They dream of the possibility that a change of government will necessitate another such massive sitting. All are hopeful that it can come again, reasoning that people's appearances change over the years and it is foolish not to update their photographs. Indeed, there is a move afoot (supported, quite naturally, by the *ambulantes* if not actually instigated by them) to do as other Latin American countries have done and require new identification photographs every three years. It is a dream that carries them through some of their darkest hours. As with many such business bonanzas, only the memory of this one now remains. The financial gains, like those from most sudden windfalls, were quickly garnered and spent. Life today for the itinerant photographer is as hectic and uncertain as ever; it differs little from what it was before *La Época de la Cedula*.

Although signs of change weigh heavily over the world of *los ambulantes*, there is no real indication that it will come about immediately. The tradition remains strong and true. For a while yet these intrepid adventurers will be packing their gear and following the roads that lead to the next run of village fairs. Wherever celebrations are held and there are people willing to part with a few cents for photographic mementos, these men will be on hand to accommodate them.

To those who are interested in the preservation of folk traditions it is comforting to know that on this day, if not at this very moment, somewhere in the highlands of Guatemala, in some Indian-crowded marketplace or on a sidestreet or at the corner of some village square, there is an itinerant photographer with tripod and camera set up awaiting his next customer.

Los Ambulantes

Dedicated to the photographers,
without whose friendship and cooperation
this book would not have been possible.

56–57

68–69

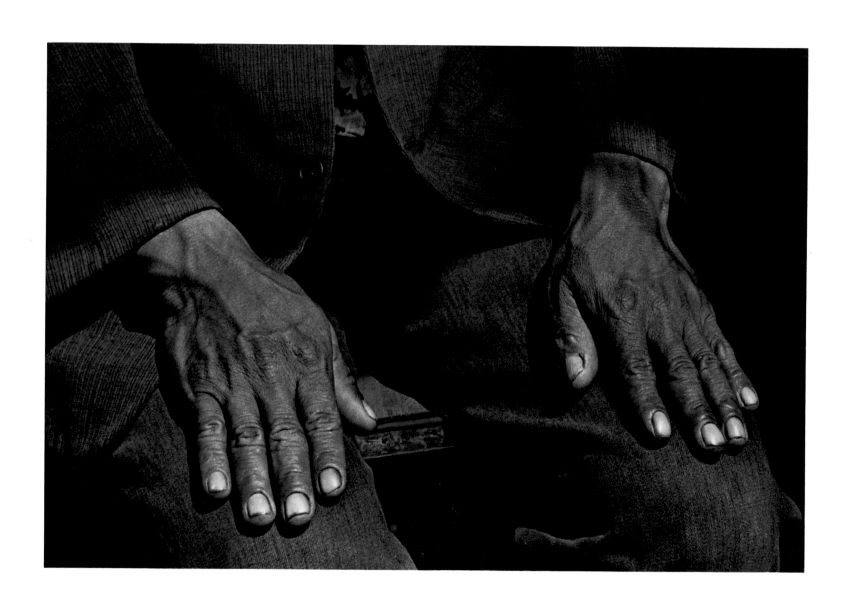

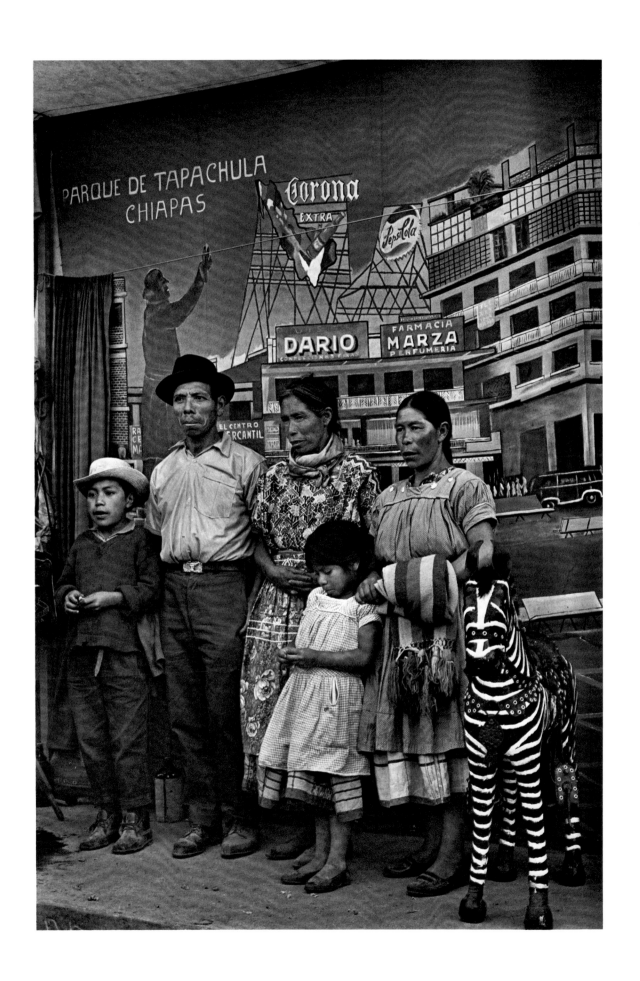

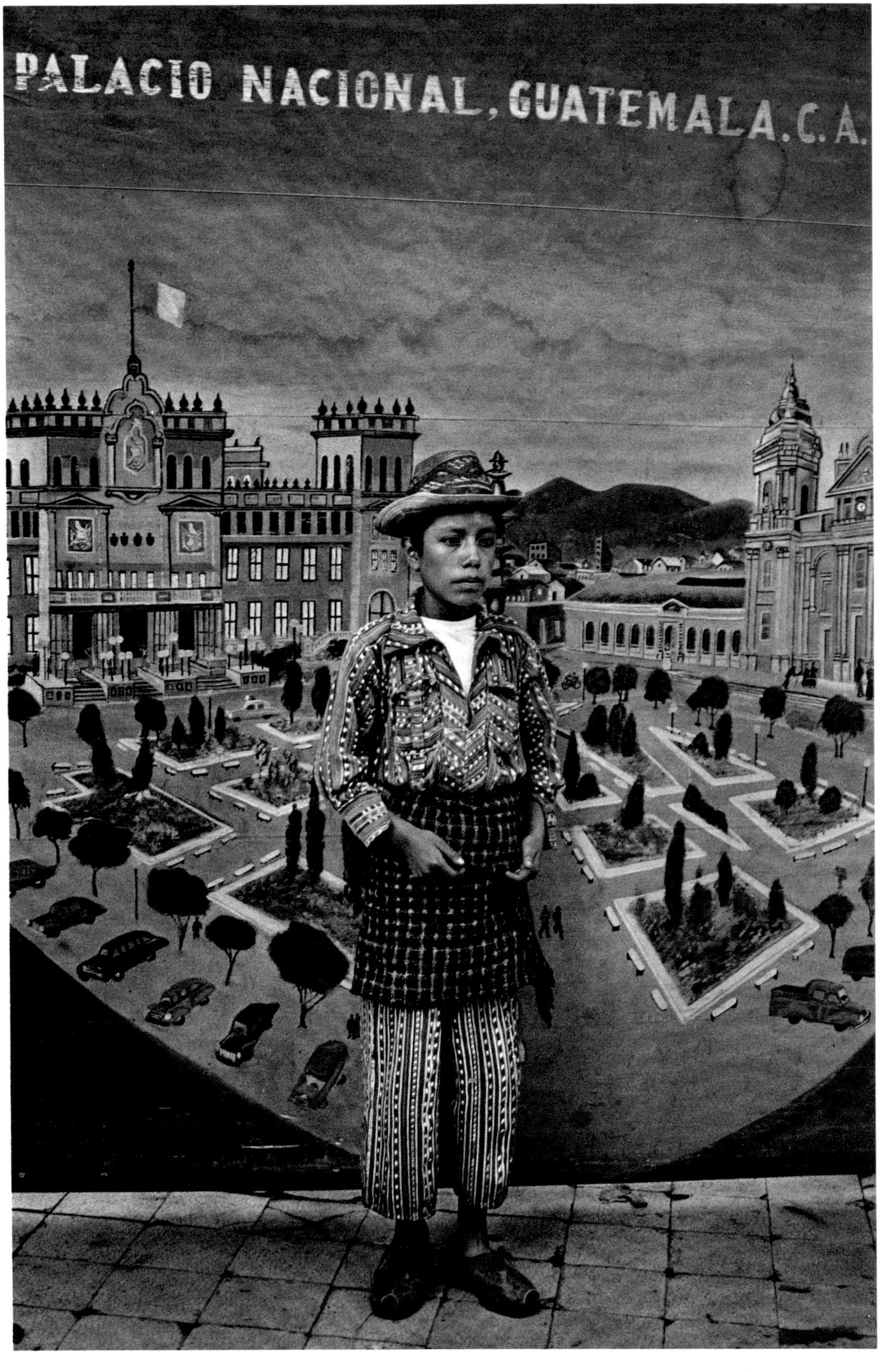
PALACIO NACIONAL, GUATEMALA. C. A.

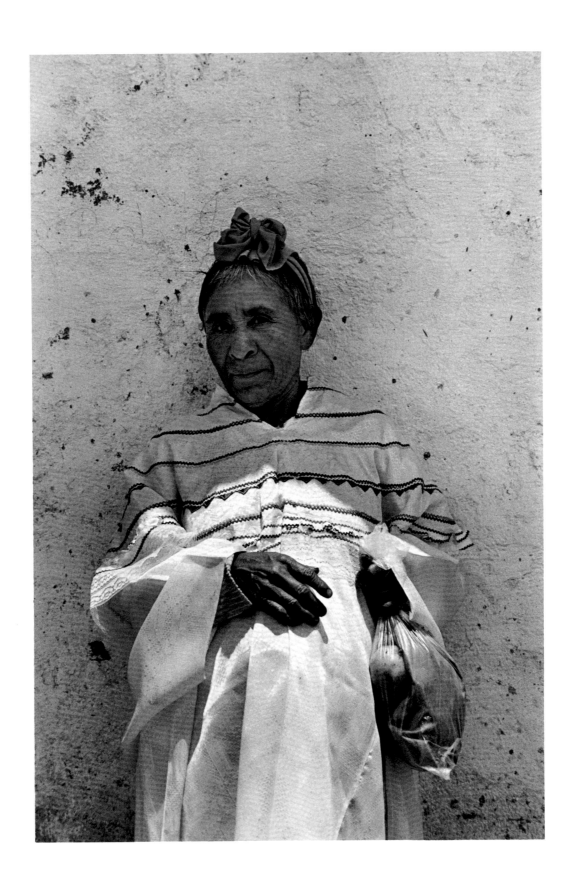

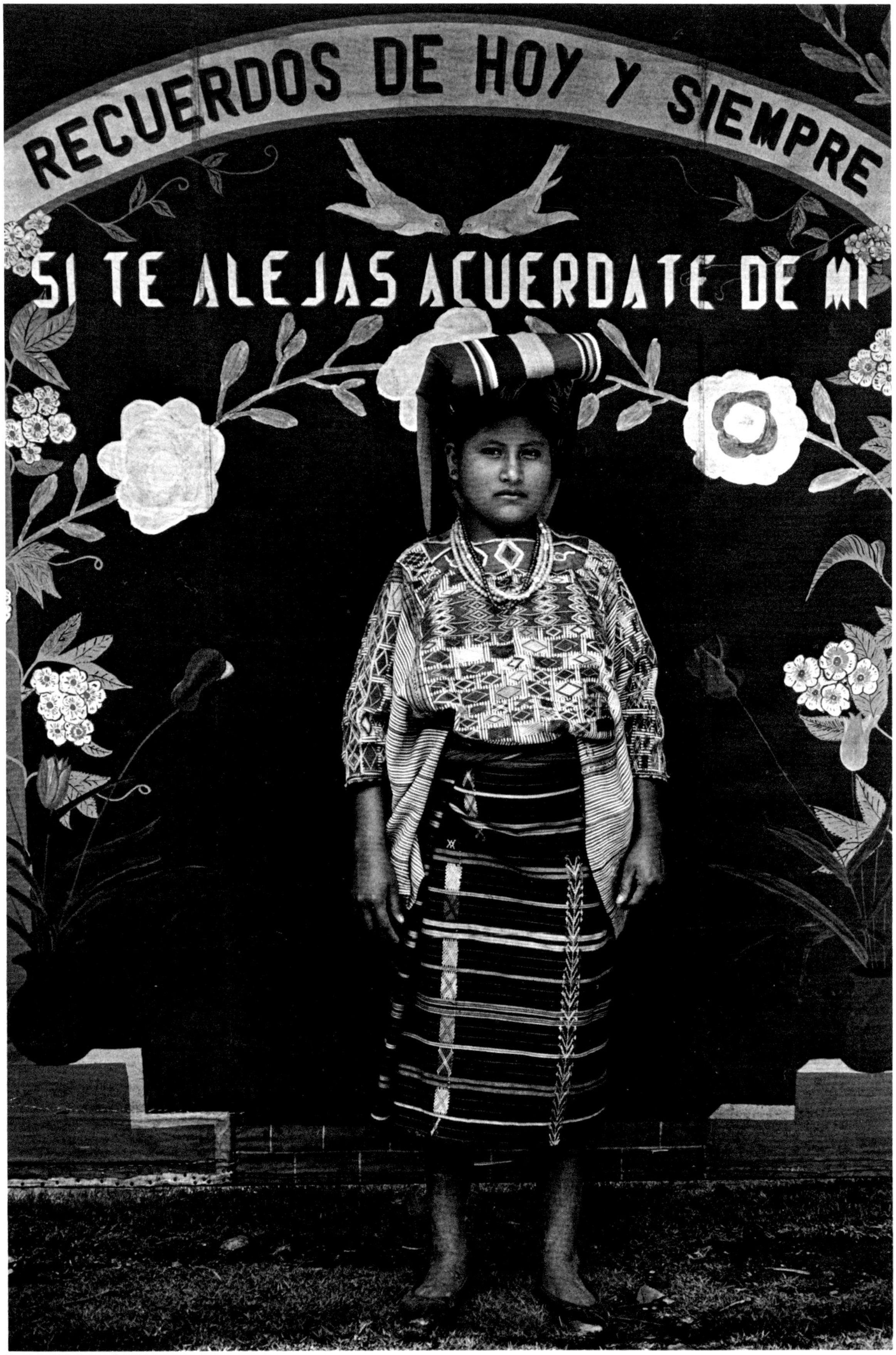
RECUERDOS DE HOY Y SIEMPRE
SI TE ALEJAS ACUERDATE DE MI

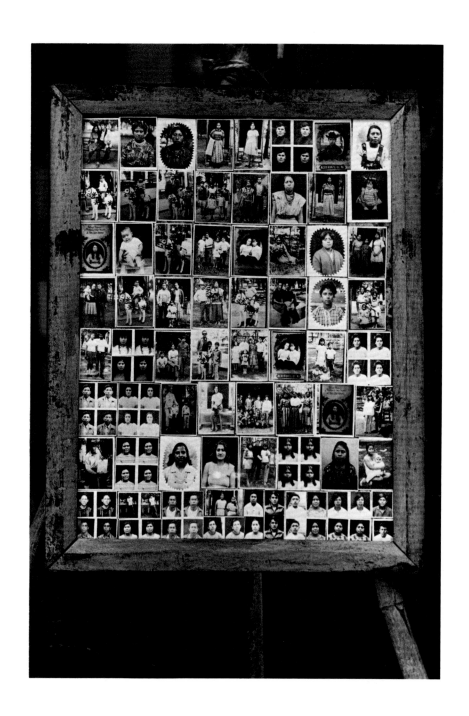

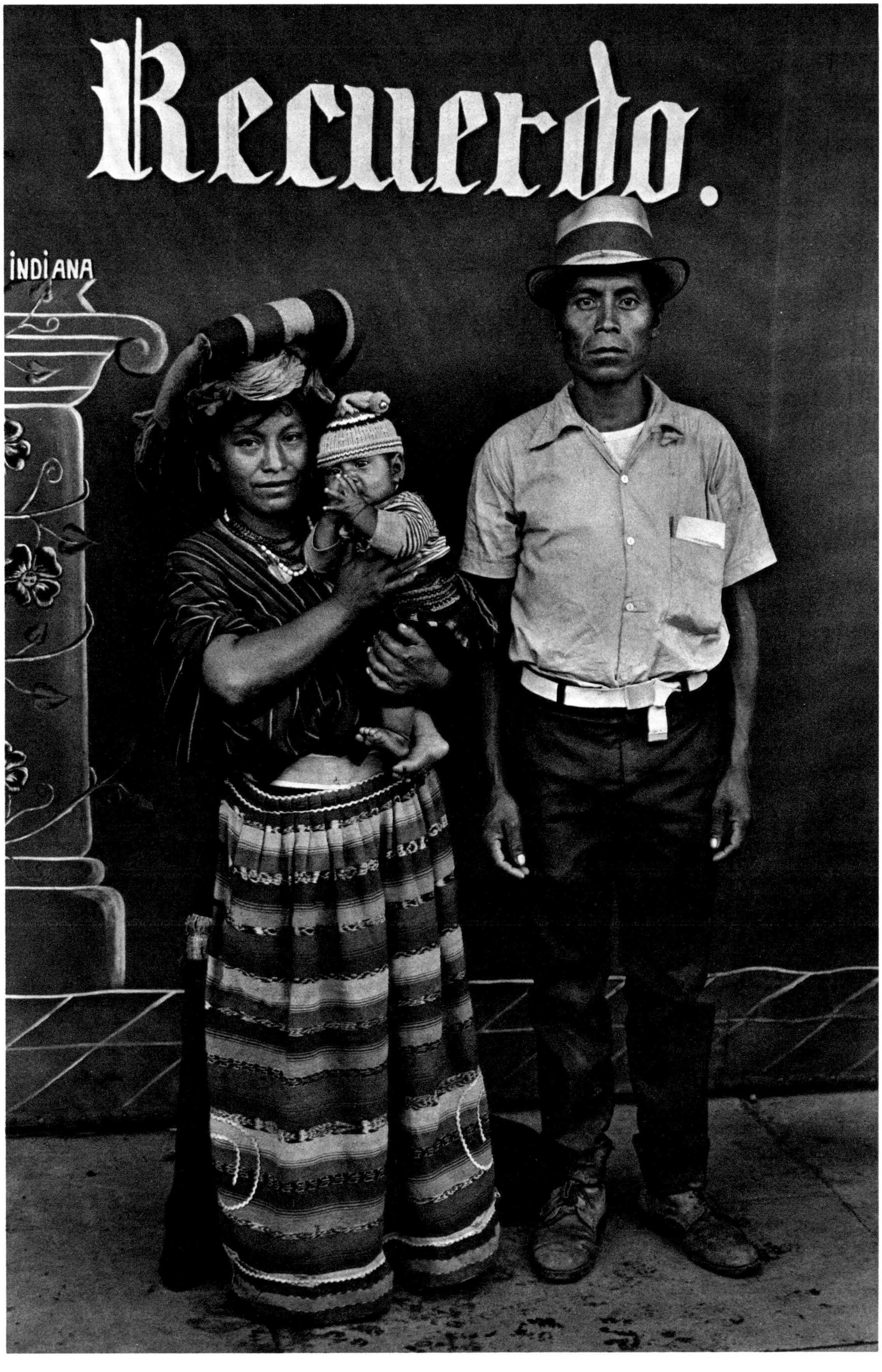
Recuerdo.
INDIANA

Legends

DATE DUE
